Spanish Short Stories for Beginners
Book 3

Over 100 Dialogues and Daily Used Phrases to Learn Spanish in Your Car. Have Fun & Grow Your Vocabulary, with Crazy Effective Language Learning Lessons

www.LearnLikeNatives.com

www.LearnLikeNatives.com

© Copyright 2020
By Learn Like A Native

ALL RIGHTS RESERVED

No part of this book may be reproduced, stored in a retrieval system, or transmitted in any form or by any means, without the prior written permission of the publisher.

www.LearnLikeNatives.com

TABLE OF CONTENT

INTRODUCTION	5
CHAPTER 1 The Car / emotions	17
Translation of the Story	35
The Car	35
CHAPTER 2 Going to A Meeting / telling time	47
Translation of the Story	63
Going to A Meeting	63
CHAPTER 3 Lunch with The Queen / to be, to have + food	75
Translation of the Story	93
Lunch with The Queen	93
CONCLUSION	105
About the Author	111

www.LearnLikeNatives.com

www.LearnLikeNatives.com

INTRODUCTION

Before we dive into some Spanish, I want to congratulate you, whether you're just beginning, continuing, or resuming your language learning journey. Here at Learn Like a Native, we understand the determination it takes to pick up a new language and after reading this book, you'll be another step closer to achieving your language goals.

As a thank you for learning with us, we are giving you free access to our 'Speak Like a Native' eBook. It's packed full of practical advice and insider tips on how to make language learning quick, easy, and most importantly, enjoyable. Head over to LearnLikeNatives.com to access your free guide and peruse our huge selection of language learning resources.

www.LearnLikeNatives.com

Learning a new language is a bit like cooking—you need several different ingredients and the right technique, but the end result is sure to be delicious. We created this book of short stories for learning Spanish because language is alive. Language is about the senses—hearing, tasting the words on your tongue, and touching another culture up close. Learning a language in a classroom is a fine place to start, but it's not a complete introduction to a language.

In this book, you'll find a language come to life. These short stories are miniature immersions into the Spanish language, at a level that is perfect for beginners. This book is not a lecture on grammar. It's not an endless vocabulary list. This book is the closest you can come to a language immersion without leaving the country. In the stories within, you will see people speaking to each other, going through daily life situations, and using the most common, helpful words and phrases in language.

www.LearnLikeNatives.com

You are holding the key to bringing your Spanish studies to life.

Made for Beginners

We made this book with beginners in mind. You'll find that the language is simple, but not boring. Most of the book is in the present tense, so you will be able to focus on dialogues, root verbs, and understand and find patterns in subject-verb agreement.

This is not "just" a translated book. While reading novels and short stories translated into Spanish is a wonderful thing, beginners (and even novices) often run into difficulty. Literary licenses and complex sentence structure can make reading in your second language truly difficult—not to mention BORING. That's why Spanish Short

Stories for Beginners is the perfect book to pick up. The stories are simple, but not infantile. They were not written for children, but the language is simple so that beginners can pick it up.

The Benefits of Learning a Second Language

If you have picked up this book, it's likely that you are already aware of the many benefits of learning a second language. Besides just being fun, knowing more than one language opens up a whole new world to you. You will be able to communicate with a much larger chunk of the world. Opportunities in the workforce will open up, and maybe even your day-to-day work will be improved. Improved communication can also help you expand your business. And from a neurological perspective, learning a second language is like taking your daily vitamins and eating well, for your brain!

How To Use The Book

The chapters of this book all follow the same structure:

- A short story with several dialogs
- A summary in Spanish
- A list of important words and phrases and their English translation
- Questions to test your understanding
- Answers to check if you were right
- The English translation of the story to clear every doubt

www.LearnLikeNatives.com

You may use this book however is comfortable for you, but we have a few recommendations for getting the most out of the experience. Try these tips and if they work for you, you can use them on every chapter throughout the book.

1) Start by reading the story all the way through. Don't stop or get hung up on any particular words or phrases. See how much of the plot you can understand in this way. We think you'll get a lot more of it than you may expect, but it is completely normal not to understand everything in the story. You are learning a new language, and that takes time.

2) Read the summary in Spanish. See if it matches what you have understood of the plot.

www.LearnLikeNatives.com

3) Read the story through again, slower this time. See if you can pick up the meaning of any words or phrases you don't understand by using context clues and the information from the summary.

4) Test yourself! Try to answer the five comprehension questions that come at the end of each story. Write your answers down, and then check them against the answer key. How did you do? If you didn't get them all, no worries!

5) Look over the vocabulary list that accompanies the chapter. Are any of these the words you did not understand? Did you already know the meaning of some of them from your reading?

6) Now go through the story once more. Pay attention this time to the words and phrases you haven't understand. If you'd like, take the time to look them up to

expand your meaning of the story. Every time you read over the story, you'll understand more and more.

7) Move on to the next chapter when you are ready.

Read and Listen

The audio version is the best way to experience this book, as you will hear a native Spanish speaker tell you each story. You will become accustomed to their accent as you listen along, a huge plus for when you want to apply your new language skills in the real world.

If this has ignited your language learning passion and you are keen to find out what other resources are available, go to LearnLikeNatives.com,

www.LearnLikeNatives.com

where you can access our vast range of free learning materials. Don't know where to begin? An excellent place to start is our 'Speak Like a Native' free eBook, full of practical advice and insider tips on how to make language learning quick, easy, and most importantly, enjoyable.

And remember, small steps add up to great advancements! No moment is better to begin learning than the present.

www.LearnLikeNatives.com

FREE BOOK!

Get the *FREE BOOK* that reveals the secrets path to learn any language fast, and without leaving your country.

Discover:

- The **language 5 golden rules** to master languages at will

- Proven **mind training techniques** to revolutionize your learning

- A complete step-by-step guide to **conquering any language**

www.LearnLikeNatives.com

www.LearnLikeNatives.com

www.LearnLikeNatives.com

CHAPTER 1
The Car / emotions

HISTORIA

Quentin está **interesado** en los coches. Mira las fotos de los coches. Lee sobre los coches toda la noche, todas las noches. Cuando se **aburre**, navega a través de Instagram. Las cuentas que sigue tratan de coches.

La novia de Quentin es Rashel. Rashel se **divierte** por la obsesión de Quentin. Los coches no le interesan.

Quentin tiene un coche. Conduce un Honda Accord 2000. Es verde. Quentin se siente avergonzado por su coche. Quiere un coche fresco.

Quiere un coche para conducir por la ciudad con Rashel. Sueña con coches bonitos y caros. Quiere un coche grande. Los pequeños son aburridos.

Últimamente, Quentin mira su teléfono todo el tiempo. Cuando Rashel lo mira, Quentin esconde el teléfono.

"Quentin, ¿por qué me ocultas el teléfono?", pregunta Rashel.

"Por ninguna razón", dice Quentin.

"¡Eso no es verdad!", dice Rashel.

"¡Lo prometo!", dice Quentin.

"Entonces déjame ver la pantalla", dice Rashel.

"No es nada", dice Quentin. "Olvídalo."

Rashel está **sospechando**. Quentin está ocultando algo.

Una noche, Rashel hace la cena. Suena el teléfono de Quentin. Ella no sabe el número. Quentin contesta el teléfono.

"¿Hola? Oh. Te llamaré más tarde", dice Quentin. Cuelga.

"¿Quién es?", dice Rashel.

"Nadie", dice Quentin.

"¿Es una chica?" pregunta Rashel. Está **celosa**.

"No, no lo es", dice Quentin.

"¿Entonces quién es?", pregunta Rashel.

"Nadie", dice Quentin.

"¿Por qué no me lo dices?", pregunta Rashel.

Está tan **enojado**, Quentin sale de la casa. Deja la comida sobre la mesa. Hace frío. Rashel está **triste**. La cena es un desperdicio. Rashel llama a su amigo. Hablan de la cena. El amigo de Rashel piensa que Quentin está con otra chica. Rashel no está segura. Quentin está escondiendo algo. De eso si está segura.

Quentin se sienta en su coche. Abre su portátil. Busca anuncios de coches de segunda mano. Hay coches baratos y coches caros. Tiene

esperanzas. Busca un coche que sea una buena ganga. Tiene un poco de dinero. Él y Rashel ahorrar dinero. Lo utilizan para las vacaciones. Este año, Quentin quiere un coche, no unas vacaciones.

Ve un anuncio sobre un coche viejo. El coche es del año 1990. El coche es un Jeep. El modelo es un Grand Wagoneer. Siente **curiosidad** por el coche. Ningún coche se parece a este coche. Tiene madera en el exterior. Quentin piensa que es fresco.

Quentin llama al número del anuncio.

"Hola", dice un hombre.

"Hola", dice Quentin. "Estoy llamando por el coche."

"¿Qué coche?" pregunta el hombre.

"El Jeep", dice Quentin. "Me lo llevo."

"Ok", dice el hombre.

"Iré a buscarlo mañana", dice Quentin.

"¡Ok!", dice el hombre. Cuelga el teléfono.

Quentin vuelve a la casa. Se siente **culpable**. La cena está fría. Se la come de todos modos. Está nervioso. ¿Qué pensará Rashel del coche?

Al día siguiente, Quentin consigue el coche. Quentin ama el coche nuevo. Su coche es un Jeep Grand Wagoneer 1990. Es un coche grande. Tiene paneles de madera a lo largo del lado.

Quentin conduce a la casa. El coche tiene 120.000 kilómetros. Tiene unos 30 años. El coche está en muy buenas condiciones. Todo funciona. El interior es como nuevo. El nuevo coche de Quentin es especial. No se siente **avergonzado** de conducir. Por el contrario, se siente **orgulloso** de conducir por la ciudad. ¿Qué más se puede pedir?

Llama a la puerta. Rashel la abre.

"Rashel", dice. "¡Mira!" Quentin apunta al coche.

"¿Tienes un auto nuevo?", pregunta.

"Sí", dice Quentin. Invita a Rashel a montar. Los dos conducen por la ciudad. Quentin conduce lento. Mucha gente mira fijamente al coche. Es un coche especial. Varios hombres parecen

envidiarlo. Quieren un coche fresco. Quentin es finalmente **feliz**.

Quentin pasa todos los días con el Jeep. Él lo conduce. A veces no tiene a dónde ir. Él sólo conduce alrededor de la ciudad. Le encanta el coche. Se siente **seguro** en el Jeep. Pasa todas las noches limpiando el coche. Él pule las puertas y ventanas todas las noches. Rashel lo espera. Llega tarde a cenar. Esto **enfurece** a Rashel. Odia al Jeep Wagoneer. Cree que Quentin ama más al coche que a ella. Ella le dice esto a Quentin y él le dice que no sea **estúpida**. Él le da un abrazo **amoroso**. Quiere demostrarle que está equivocada.

El sábado, Rashel y Quentin van al supermercado. Quentin lo conduce. Las ventanas están bajadas. Quentin lleva gafas de sol. Parece **confiado** y seguro de sí mismo. Aparca el coche. Los dos van al supermercado.

Ellos van a comprar la fruta.

"Quentin, ¿puedes conseguir cuatro manzanas?" pregunta Rashel. Quentin va a buscar la fruta. Regresa. Pero tiene cuatro naranjas.

"¡Quentin, dije manzanas!", dice Rashel.

"Sí, lo sé", dice Quentin.

"¡Son naranjas!", dice Rashel.

"Oh, lo siento", dice Quentin. Está **distraído**. No puede concentrarse.

"¿Qué pasa?", pregunta Rashel.

"Nada", dice Quentin.

"¿En qué estás pensando?", pregunta.

"Nada", dice Quentin. Tiene una mirada **ansiosa**. Tiene una mirada de **preocupación** en sus ojos.

"¿Estás pensando en el coche?", pregunta Rashel.

"No", dice Quentin.

"¡Sí! ¡Lo sé! Ve y tráeme unas manzanas", dice Rashel. Está decidida a hacer que Quentin preste atención. Quentin trae las manzanas. Las pone en el carrito. Terminan de comprar comida. Quentin está tranquilo. Parece **retraído**. Van al coche.

El estacionamiento está lleno. Quentin inspecciona el Jeep con cuidado. Tiene **miedo** de marcas o arañazos. La puerta de un coche deja marcas cuando golpea otra puerta. Hay muchos coches ahora. Él no ve ningún rasguño. Quentin abre el coche. Él entra.

Rashel pone los comestibles en el coche. Ella devuelve el carro a la tienda. Ella abre la puerta y entra.

"Quentin, soy **miserable**", dice. Está llorando.

"¿Qué?", dice Quentin. Está **sorprendido**. ¿Qué pasa?

"Sólo te importa el coche", dice Rashel.

"Eso no es verdad", dice Quentin.

"No me ayudas a hacer nada", dice Rashel.

"¡Sí! Me preocupo por ti", dice Quentin.

"Si te importo, vende este coche", dice Rashel.

RESUMEN

Quentin quiere un coche nuevo. Oculta su búsqueda de su novia Rashel. Ella le pregunta quién llama, qué está mirando. Pero Quentin mantiene su búsqueda en secreto. Quentin encuentra un coche que ama. Finalmente es feliz. Sin embargo, está demasiado obsesionado con el coche. Rashel se pone celosa. Quentin no puede concentrarse en la tienda de comestibles. Le preocupa que alguien va a rayar el coche. Quentin no ayuda a Rashel con las compras. Ella se enoja. Ella le dice a Quentin que debe elegir entre ella y el coche.

www.LearnLikeNatives.com

Lista de Vocabulario

interested	interesado
bored	aburrido
amused	entretenido
suspicious	suspicaz
embarrassed	avergonzado
jealous	celoso
angry	enojado
sad	triste
hopeful	esperanzado
curious	curioso
guilty	culpable
nervous	nervioso
ashamed	avergonzado
proud	orgulloso
envious	envidioso

happy	feliz
enraged	enfurecido
stupid	estúpido
loving	cariñoso
confident	confiado
distracted	distraído
anxious	ansioso
worried	preocupado
determined	determinado
withdrawn	retraido
miserable	miserable
surprised	sorprendido

www.LearnLikeNatives.com

PREGUNTAS

1) ¿Qué piensa Quentin de su coche al principio de la historia?

    a) él lo ama

    b) se siente avergonzado por él

    c) es demasiado nuevo

    d) es demasiado caro

2) ¿Por qué Rashel se enoja en la cena?

    a) ella piensa que una chica está llamando a Quentin

    b) ella tiene hambre

    c) Quentin está atrasado

    d) Quentin olvidó comprar pan

3) ¿Qué hace Quentin en la tienda de comestibles?

a) paga por todo

b) obtiene naranjas en lugar de manzanas

c) él derrama leche

d) presta atención a Rashel

4) ¿Qué piensa Quentin de su nuevo coche?

a) es demasiado nuevo

b) es demasiado pequeño

c) está orgulloso de él

d) se siente avergonzado por él

5) Al final de la historia, Quentin y Rashel:

a) se besan

b) disimulan una pelea

c) salen de la tienda

d) tienen una pelea

www.LearnLikeNatives.com

RESPUESTAS

1) ¿Qué piensa Quentin de su coche al principio de la historia?

    b) se siente avergonzado por él

2) ¿Por qué Rashel se enoja en la cena?

    a) ella piensa que una chica está llamando a Quentin

3) ¿Qué hace Quentin en la tienda de comestibles?

    b) obtiene naranjas en lugar de manzanas

4) ¿Qué piensa Quentin de su nuevo coche?

    c) está orgulloso de él

5) Al final de la historia, Quentin y Rashel:

d) tienen una pelea

www.LearnLikeNatives.com

Translation of the Story

The Car

STORY

Quentin is **interested** in cars. He looks at pictures of cars. He reads about cars all night, every night. When he is **bored**, he scrolls through Instagram. The accounts he follows are all about cars.

Quentin's girlfriend is Rashel. Rashel is **amused** by Quentin's obsession. Cars do not interest her.

Quentin has a car. Quentin drives a 2000 Honda Accord. His car is green. Quentin feels **embarrassed** by his car. He wants a cool car. He wants a car to drive around town with Rashel. He dreams of nice cars, expensive cars. He wants a big car. Small cars are boring.

Lately, Quentin looks at his phone all the time. When Rashel looks at it, Quentin hides the phone.

"Quentin, why do you hide the phone from me?" asks Rashel.

"No reason," says Quentin.

"That's not true!" says Rashel.

"I promise it is!" says Quentin.

"Then let me see the screen," says Rashel.

"It's nothing," says Quentin. "Forget about it."

Rashel is **suspicious**. Quentin is hiding something.

One night, Rashel makes dinner. Quentin's phone rings. She does not know the number. Quentin answers the phone.

"Hello? Oh. I will call you later," says Quentin. He hangs up.

"Who is it?" says Rashel.

"Nobody," says Quentin.

"Is it a girl?" asks Rashel. She is **jealous**.

"No it is not," says Quentin.

"Then who is it?" asks Rashel.

"Nobody," says Quentin.

"Why won't you tell me?" asks Rashel.

He is so **angry**; Quentin walks out of the house. He leaves the food on the table. It gets cold. Rashel is **sad**. The dinner is a waste. Rashel calls her friend. They talk about the dinner. Rashel's friend thinks Quentin is with another girl. Rashel is unsure. Quentin is hiding something. She is sure.

Quentin sits in his car. He opens his laptop. He searches adverts for second-hand cars. There are cheap cars and expensive cars. He is **hopeful**. He looks for a car that is a good bargain. He has a little money. He and Rashel save money. They use it for vacation. This year, Quentin wants a car, not a vacation.

He sees an advert about an old car. The car is from the year 1990. The car is a Jeep. The model is a Grand Wagoneer. He is **curious** about the car. No cars look like this car. It has wood on the outside. Quentin thinks that is cool.

Quentin calls the number on the advert.

"Hello," says a man.

"Hello," says Quentin. "I am calling about the car."

"Which car?" asks the man.

"The Jeep," says Quentin. "I'll take it."

"Ok," says the man.

"I'll come get it tomorrow," says Quentin.

"Ok!" says the man. He hangs up the phone.

Quentin goes back to the house. He feels **guilty**. Dinner is cold. He eats it anyway. He is **nervous**. What will Rashel think about the car?

The next day, Quentin gets the car. Quentin loves the new car. His car is a 1990 Jeep Grand Wagoneer. It is a big car. It has wood panels along the side.

Quentin drives to the house. The car has 120,000 kilometers. It is about 30 years old. The car is in very good condition. Everything works. The interior is like new. Quentin's new car is special. He does not feel **ashamed** driving. On the contrary, he feels **proud** driving through town. What is not to love?

He knocks on the door. Rashel opens it.

"Rashel," he says. "Look!" Quentin points at the car.

"You have a new car?" she asks.

"Yes," says Quentin. He invites Rashel to ride. The two drive around town. Quentin drives slow. Many people stare at the car. It is a special car.

Several men look **envious**. They want a cool car. Quentin is finally **happy**.

Quentin spends every day with the Jeep. He drives it. Sometimes he has nowhere to go. He just drives around town. He loves the car. He feels **confident** in the Jeep. He spends every evening cleaning the car. He polishes the doors and windows every night. Rashel waits for him. He is late for dinner. This makes Rashel **enraged**. She hates the Jeep Wagoneer. She thinks Quentin loves the car more than he loves her. She tells Quentin this and he tells her not to be **stupid**. He gives her a **loving** hug. He wants to show her she is wrong.

On Saturday, Rashel and Quentin go to the supermarket. Quentin drives them. The windows are down. Quentin wears sunglasses. He looks **confident** and sure of himself. He parks the car. The two go into the supermarket.

They shop for fruit.

"Quentin, can you get four apples?" asks Rashel. Quentin goes to get the fruit. He returns. But he has four oranges.

"Quentin, I said apples!" says Rashel.

"Yeah, I know," says Quentin.

"These are oranges!" says Rashel.

"Oh, sorry," says Quentin. He is **distracted**. He cannot concentrate.

"What is wrong?" asks Rashel.

"Nothing," says Quentin.

"What are you thinking about?" she asks.

"Nothing," says Quentin. He has an **anxious** look. He has a **worried** look in his eyes.

"Are you thinking about the car?" asks Rashel.

"No," says Quentin.

"Yes you are! I know it! Go get me some apples," says Rashel. She is **determined** to make Quentin pay attention. Quentin brings back the apples. He puts them in the cart. They finish grocery shopping. Quentin is quiet. He seems **withdrawn**. They go to the car.

The parking lot is full. Quentin inspects the Jeep carefully. He is **afraid** of marks or scratches. A car door leaves marks when it hits another door. There are many cars now. He does not see any scratches. Quentin unlocks the car. He gets in.

Rashel puts the groceries in the car. She returns the cart to the store. She opens the door and gets in.

"Quentin, I am **miserable**," she says. She is crying.

"What?" says Quentin. He is **surprised**. What is wrong?

"You only care about the car," says Rashel.

"That's not true," says Quentin.

"You don't help me do anything," says Rashel.

"I do! I care about you," says Quentin.

"If you care about me, sell this car," says Rashel.

www.LearnLikeNatives.com

CHAPTER 2
Going to A Meeting / telling time

HISTORIA

Thomas sale de su apartamento. Es un día hermoso. El sol brilla. El aire es fresco. Thomas tiene una reunión importante hoy. Thomas es el CEO de una empresa. Hoy se reúne con nuevos inversores. Está preparado para la reunión. Se siente relajado.

Son las **ocho de la mañana**. Thomas camina por la calle de la ciudad. Es temprano. Quiere **tiempo** extra. No quiere llegar tarde. Él no quiere estresarse.

Thomas vive en una gran ciudad. Hay edificios altos por todas partes. Pasan taxis. Pasan muchos coches. A Thomas le gusta caminar. A veces toma el metro.

Thomas quiere desayunar. Se detiene en un café. El café es relajante. La música suena. Thomas quiere algo bueno al horno.

"¿Qué te gustaría?", pregunta el barista.

"Un panecillo por favor", dice Thomas.

"¿Arándanos o chocolate?" pregunta la barista.

"Arándanos, por favor", dice Thomas.

"¿Algo de beber?" pregunta la barista.

"Un café", dice Thomas.

"¿Negro?", pregunta el barista.

"No, con un poco de crema", dice.

"¿Para llevar?", pregunta el barista. Thomas mira su reloj. Son las **ocho y media**. Tiene tiempo.

"Para tomar aquí", dice Thomas. Se sienta y come. Ve pasar a la gente. Thomas mira su reloj de nuevo. Son las **nueve en punto**. Se levanta. Thomas tira la basura y va al baño. Se quita el reloj para lavarse las manos. Su reloj es de oro y no le gusta que se moje. Su teléfono está sonando.

"Hola", dice Thomas.

"Señor, ¿está en la oficina?" pregunta la secretaria de Thomas.

"Todavía no", dice Thomas. "Voy en camino."

Sale de la cafetería. Thomas camina hacia el metro. Tiene tiempo, así que no necesita un taxi. Mira su reloj de nuevo. Pero su reloj no está ahí. Thomas siente pánico. Piensa en la mañana. ¿Lo dejó en casa? No. Recuerda que se quitó el reloj y se lavó las manos. El reloj está en la cafetería.

Thomas vuelve a la cafetería.

"Disculpe", le dice al barista.

"¿Tienes un reloj de oro?", pregunta.

"Deme un **segundo**", dice el barista. Le pregunta a sus colegas. Nadie tiene el reloj.

"No", dice el barista. Thomas va al baño. Mira por el lavabo. El reloj no está ahí. Alguien tiene el reloj, piensa Thomas. Ya no tiene tiempo de buscar.

"Disculpe", le dice al barista otra vez.

"¿Qué hora es?", pregunta.

"Diez y nueve a.m." dice la barista.

"Gracias", dice Thomas. Thomas se apresura. Tiene la reunión a las once menos cuarto. Corre a la parada del metro. Hay una larga cola para comprar tickets. Espera durante cinco **minutos**.

"¿Tienes la hora?" le pregunta Thomas a una mujer.

"Son las diez y **treinta**", dice. Thomas llega tarde. Sale de la línea larga. Va a la calle. Saluda a un taxi. Todos los taxis están llenos. Finalmente, un taxi se detiene. Thomas entra en el taxi.

"¿A dónde vas?" pregunta el conductor.

"A la 116 con Park", dice Thomas.

"Ok", dice el conductor.

"Por favor, date prisa", dice Thomas. "Necesito **estar a tiempo** para una reunión."

"Sí, señor", dice el conductor.

Thomas llega a la oficina. Sale corriendo del taxi y sube las escaleras. Su secretaria le dice hola. ¡Thomas está sudoroso!

"Señor, la reunión es ahora en **una hora**", dice la secretaria. Thomas limpia el sudor de su cara.

"Bien", dice Thomas. Se prepara para la reunión. Su camisa está sudada. Huele mal. Thomas decide comprar una camisa nueva para la reunión.

Thomas va a la tienda calle abajo.

"Hola, señor", dice la vendedora. "¿Cómo podemos ayudarle?"

"Necesito una camisa nueva", dice Thomas. La vendedora lleva a Thomas a ver las camisas. Hay camisas rosadas, marrones, a cuadros, y de rayas.

El vendedor habla mucho. Thomas está nervioso por la hora.

"¿Qué hora es?", le pregunta Thomas a la vendedora.

"Es casi **mediodía**", dice la vendedora.

"Ok", dice Thomas. "Dame la camisa marrón." La vendedora lleva la camisa marrón a la caja registradora. Ella dobla la camisa. Y se **toma su tiempo**.

El teléfono de Thomas suena. Es su esposa.

"Cariño, cenamos a las **siete p.m.**", dice.

"Ok, querida", dice Thomas. "No puedo hablar ahora."

"Ok", dice ella. "No quiero que vuelvas a casa a las **nueve de la noche.**"

"No te preocupes", dice Thomas.

"Adiós", dice su esposa. Thomas cuelga el teléfono.

"Disculpe", dice Thomas. "Tengo prisa. No necesito la camisa envuelta."

"Bien", dice ella. Thomas paga y sale de la tienda. Se cambia de camisa mientras camina por la calle. La gente mira fijamente. Corre a la oficina.

"**Ya era hora**", dice su secretaria cuando entra. Están esperando en la reunión. Los inversores se sientan alrededor de la mesa. Thomas dice hola.

"Me gusta tu camisa, Thomas", dice uno de los inversores.

"Gracias", dice Thomas. "Es nueva." Thomas apaga su teléfono y enciende su ordenador.

"Gracias por venir", dice Thomas. "Tengo una presentación. Dura unos quince minutos."

Thomas se dirige a su secretaria. "¿Qué hora es?"

"Son las **doce y quince**", dice.

"Gracias", dice Thomas. "Falta mi reloj."

"¿Por qué no miras tu teléfono por un tiempo?", dice uno de los inversores.

"Por supuesto", dice Thomas. ¡Está tan acostumbrado a su reloj que olvida que puede mirar el teléfono por el momento!

"Debo ser la última persona en el mundo que sólo usa un reloj para **decir la hora**", dice Thomas. Todo el mundo se ríe.

RESUMEN

Thomas comienza su día con mucho tiempo. Desayuna y se relaja. Va al baño y deja su reloj en el baño. Cuando se da cuenta, vuelve a la cafetería. El reloj no estaba. Ahora debe preguntar a todos qué hora es. Llega tarde a la oficina. Afortunadamente, su reunión se pospone una hora. Va a comprar una camisa nueva. Eso toma más tiempo del que espera. Corre a la reunión. Cuando pide la hora, de nuevo, se da cuenta de que sólo podía mirar su teléfono por el momento. La reunión comienza.

Lista de Vocabulario

It is ___ o'clock	Son las ___ en punto
in the morning	por la mañana
time	tiempo
half past ___	___ y media
on the dot	en punto
second	segundo
What time is it?	¿Y qué hora es?
___ oh ___	___ y ___
a.m.	a.m.

www.LearnLikeNatives.com

a quarter to _____	un cuarto para las ____
minutes	minutos
Do you have the time?	¿Tienes la hora?
____ thirty	____ y treinta
on time	a tiempo
in an hour	en una hora
What's the time?	¿Cuál es la hora?
nearly	temprano
noon	mediodía
takes her time	tomar su tiempo
p.m.	p.m.
at night	de la noche
about time	sobre el tiempo
____ minutes long	____ minutos de largo
____ fifteen	____ y quince
tell the time	decir la hora

PREGUNTAS

1) ¿Por qué Thomas pierde su reloj?

   a) Se le cae

   b) Deja que un extraño lo sostenga

   c) Hace una apuesta

   d) Se lo quita para lavarse las manos

2) ¿Dónde vive Thomas?

   a) en un pueblo pequeño

   b) en una ciudad con poco transporte

   c) en una gran ciudad

   d) en el campo

3) Thomas tiene suerte porque:

   a) tiene buenos compañeros de trabajo

b) se aplaza su reunión

c) el metro no está ocupado

d) no pierde su reloj

4) Thomas le dice a la vendedora que no envuelva la camisa porque:

a) llega tarde a su reunión

b) se ve el sudor en su camisa

c) su esposa espera en el teléfono

d) odia desperdiciar bolsas

5) Todos se ríen al final de la historia porque:

a) La camisa de Thomas está sudada

b) Thomas está avergonzado

c) Thomas olvida que se puede saber la hora con el teléfono

d) Thomas pierde su reloj.

www.LearnLikeNatives.com

RESPUESTAS

1) ¿Por qué Thomas pierde su reloj?

    d) Se lo quita para lavarse las manos

2) ¿Dónde vive Thomas?

    c) en una gran ciudad

3) Thomas tiene suerte porque:

    b) se aplaza su reunión

4) Thomas le dice a la vendedora que no envuelva la camisa porque:

    a) llega tarde a su reunión

5) Todos se ríen al final de la historia porque:

    c) Thomas olvida que se puede saber la hora con el teléfono

Translation of the Story

Going to A Meeting

STORY

Thomas leaves his apartment building. It is a beautiful day. The sun shines. The air is fresh. Thomas has an important meeting today. Thomas is the CEO of a company. Today he meets with new investors. He is prepared for the meeting. He feels relaxed.

It is **eight o'clock in the morning**. Thomas walks down the city street. He is early. He wants extra **time**. He does not want to be late. He does not want to stress.

Thomas lives in a big city. There are tall buildings everywhere. Taxis drive by. Lots of cars drive by.

Thomas likes to walk. Sometimes he takes the subway.

Thomas wants to eat breakfast. He stops at a café. The café is relaxed. Music plays. Thomas wants a baked good.

"What would you like?" asks the barista.

"A muffin please," says Thomas.

"Blueberry or chocolate?" asks the barista.

"Blueberry, please," says Thomas.

"Anything to drink?" asks the barista.

"A coffee," says Thomas.

"Black?" asks the barista.

"No, with a bit of cream," he says.

"To go?" asks the barista. Thomas looks at his watch. It is **half past eight.** He has time.

"For here," says Thomas. He sits down and eats. He watches people walk by. Thomas looks at his watch again. It is nine o'clock **on the dot**. He gets up. Thomas throws out the trash and goes to the bathroom. He takes off his watch to wash his hands. His watch is gold and he doesn't like to get it wet. His phone rings.

"Hello," says Thomas.

"Sir, are you at the office?" asks Thomas's secretary.

"Not yet," says Thomas. "I'm on my way."

He leaves the coffee shop. Thomas walks towards the subway. He has time, so he doesn't need a taxi. He looks at his watch again. But his watch is not there. Thomas feels panic. He thinks back over the morning. Did he leave it at home? No. He remembers taking off the watch and washing his hands. The watch is at the coffee shop.

Thomas runs back to the coffee shop.

"Excuse me," he says to the barista.

"Do you have a gold watch?" he asks.

"Just a **second**," says the barista. He asks his colleagues. No one has the watch.

"No," says the barista. Thomas goes to the bathroom. He looks by the sink. The watch is not there. Someone has the watch, Thomas thinks. He has no time to look any more.

"Excuse me," he says to the barista again.

"**What time is it?**" he asks.

"**Ten oh nine a.m.**" says the barista.

"Thanks," says Thomas. Thomas hurries. He has the meeting at a quarter to eleven. He rushes to the subway stop. There is a long line to buy tickets. He waits for five **minutes**.

"Do you have the time?" Thomas asks a woman.

"It's ten **thirty**," she says. Thomas is late. He leave the long line. He goes to the street. He waves for a taxi. All the taxis are full. Finally, a taxi stops. Thomas gets into the taxi.

"Where are you going?" asks the driver.

"To 116th and Park," says Thomas.

"Ok," says the driver.

"Please hurry," says Thomas. "I need to be **on time** for a meeting."

"Yes, sir," says the driver.

Thomas arrives to the office. He runs out of the taxi and up the stairs. His secretary says hello. Thomas is sweaty!

"Sir, the meeting is now **in an hour**," says the secretary. Thomas wipes the sweat off his face.

"Good," says Thomas. He prepares for the meeting. His shirt is sweaty. It smells bad. Thomas decides to buy a new shirt for the meeting.

Thomas goes to the store down the street.

"Hi, sir," says the salesperson. "How can we help you?"

"I need a new dress shirt," says Thomas. The salesperson takes Thomas to see the shirts. There are pink shirts, brown shirts, checked shirts, and plaid shirts. The salesperson talks a lot. Thomas is nervous about the time.

"**What's the time?**" Thomas asks the salesperson.

"It's **nearly noon**," says the salesperson.

"Ok," says Thomas. "Give me the brown shirt." The salesperson takes the brown shirt to the cash register. She folds the shirt. She **takes her time**.

Thomas's phone rings. It is his wife.

"Honey, we have dinner at seven **p.m.**," she says.

"Ok, dear," says Thomas. "I can't really talk right now."

"Ok," she says. "I just don't want you to come home at nine o'clock **at night**."

"Don't worry," says Thomas.

"Bye," says his wife. Thomas hangs up the phone.

"Excuse me," says Thomas. "I'm in a hurry. I don't need the shirt wrapped."

"Ok," she says. Thomas pays and leaves the store. He changes his shirt as he walks down the street. People stare. He hurries to the office.

"It's **about time**," says his secretary when he walks in. They are waiting in the meeting. The investors sit around the table. Thomas says hello.

"I like your shirt, Thomas," says one of the investors.

"Thanks," says Thomas. "It is new." Thomas sets his phone down and turns on his computer.

"Thank you for coming," says Thomas. "I have a presentation. It is about fifteen minutes long."

Thomas turns to his secretary. "What time is it?"

"It is **twelve fifteen**," she says.

"Thanks," says Thomas. "My watch is missing."

"Why don't you look at your phone for the time?" says one of the investors.

"Of course," says Thomas. He is so accustomed to his watch that he forgets he can look at the phone for the time!

"I must be the last person in the world to only use a watch to **tell the time**," says Thomas. Everyone laughs.

www.LearnLikeNatives.com

CHAPTER 3
Lunch with The Queen / to be, to have + food

HISTORIA

Ursula **es** una niña. Vive en Londres, Inglaterra. Estudia en la escuela. Le encanta hornear. **Tiene** una obsesión: la familia real. Quiere **ser** una princesa.

Una noche, Úrsula está en casa. Su madre prepara la cena. **Tienen** algo nuevo. Su madre lleva el plato a la mesa.

"¿Qué **son** esos?", pregunta Ursula.

"Son **puerros**", dice la mamá de Ursula.

"Oh, no me gustan los puerros", dice Ursula.

"Pruébalos", dice su madre. Los prueba. Casi vomita.

"**Estoy** enferma", dice Úrsula.

"No, no lo estas", dice su madre.

"Por favor, dame algún otro **vegetal**", dice Úrsula. "¿**Zanahorias, brócoli, ensalada**?"

"Oh, Úrsula, entonces **come** tu carne", dice su madre. Enciende la televisión. Ven las noticias. El reportaje es sobre la Reina de Inglaterra. Ursula deja de comer. Presta mucha atención.

"Reina Isabel reina en Inglaterra durante 68 años", dice el informe de noticias. "Ella está casada con el príncipe Felipe. Tienen cuatro hijos."

El reportaje habla de la Reina. Vive en el Palacio de Buckingham. Está muy sana, a pesar de su edad.

"Quiero visitar el Palacio de Buckingham", dice Ursula.

"Sí, querida", dice su madre. Ven el programa. El programa anuncia una competencia especial. Una persona puede ganar una visita al Palacio de Buckingham. El ganador almorzará con la reina. Ursula grita.

"¡**Tengo** que ganar!", grita.

"No lo sé", dice su madre. "Mucha gente participa en el concurso."

Ursula mira el programa. Aprende cómo entrar. Toma una foto de sí misma comiendo. Luego la publica en las redes sociales. Ella mira el programa, que habla de comer con la Reina. Observa como muestran lo que le pasó a un príncipe del Pacífico Sur.

La Reina está en un barco con el príncipe. Sirven el postre. El príncipe olvida vigilar a la Reina. Él toma algunas **uvas** y algunas **cerezas** de la **fruta** en la mesa y las pone en su tazón. Él vierte la **crema** sobre ellas. Espolvorea el **azúcar** en la parte superior. Empieza a comer, y luego se da cuenta de que la Reina no. Comete un gran error. La Reina toma su cuchara. Ella come un poco. Eso hace que el príncipe se sienta mejor. Está muy avergonzado.

"¿Hay reglas para comer con la Reina?", le pregunta a su madre.

"Por supuesto", dice su madre.

"¿Cómo cuál?", pregunta Ursula.

"Bueno, la Reina comienza la **comida** y termina la comida", dice la madre de Úrsula.

"Quieres decir que no puedes comer hasta que ella lo haga", dice Ursula.

"Así es", dice su madre. "Y cuando termine, tú también terminas."

"¿Y si no terminas?", pregunta Úrsula.

"Lo haces", dice su madre. "Y debes esperar a que la Reina se siente."

"¿Antes de sentarse?" dice Ursula.

"Correcto", dice su madre. Ursula piensa en esto. Hay muchas reglas si eres reina o princesa. Ursula y su madre terminan la cena. Se van a la cama.

A la mañana siguiente, Ursula se despierta. Está nerviosa por el concurso. Hoy anuncian al ganador. **Desayuna** con su madre.

"Estoy nerviosa", dice ella.

"Ursula, no vas a ganar", dice su madre. "Hay mucha gente en el concurso."

"Oh", dice Úrsula. Está triste. Come su **cereal**. No tiene hambre. Su **tocino** y sus **huevos** están intactos.

Encienden la televisión.

"Y anunciamos al ganador del Concurso del Almuerzo con la Reina", dice el hombre en la TV. Él pone su mano en un tazón de cristal enorme lleno de papeles. Mueve la mano. Saca un papel. Abre el papel.

"Y el ganador es... ¡Ursula Vann!", dice.

Ursula mira a su madre. Su madre la mira.

"¿Has oído eso?" pregunta. Su madre asiente, mirando fijamente. Su boca está abierta.

"¿He ganado?", pregunta. Su madre asiente, sin palabras.

"¡Wuu-huu!" grita Ursula. "¡Sabía que lo haría! ¡Voy a ver a la reina!" Ursula termina su comida y va a la escuela.

El día siguiente es el día para el almuerzo con la Reina. Ursula camina hasta el palacio. Está aterrorizada. Ella es sólo una niña. Esta es una gran aventura para una chica tan joven.

"¿Quién eres?", pregunta un guardia.

"Ursula Vann", dice. "Gané el concurso para almorzar con la Reina."

"Oh, hola, jovencita," dice el guardia. "Eres una jovencita bonita. Entra."

"Gracias", dice ella.

Un guardia la lleva al palacio. Es grande, muy grande. Caminan por los pasillos. El guarda tiene un sombrero divertido. Ursula se ríe. Entonces, se detiene. Están en el comedor.

¡La Reina de Inglaterra está sentada a la mesa! Delante de ella hay un plato de **sándwiches**. Es pequeña. Es feliz y sonríe.

"Hola, querida", dice ella.

"Hola, Su Majestad," dice Ursula. Ella corteja.

"Gracias por venir a almorzar", dice.

"Es un placer, Su **Majestad**", dice Úrsula.

"Espero que no te importe. Vamos a tomar **té** en lugar de un almuerzo adecuado", dice la Reina. Se sienta de nuevo. Ursula recuerda sus modales. También se sienta.

Los sándwiches son sándwiches reales, piensa. Se parecen mucho a los sándwiches de casa, sin embargo. Algunos tienen **jamón** y **queso**, con un poco de **mostaza** amarilla. Otros tienen una ensalada de **mayonesa** en ellos. Hay un plato de **galletas** al lado de algunos **bollos**.

"Perdóneme, Su Majestad", dice Úrsula.

"¿Sí, querida?", dice la Reina.

"¿Qué hay en ese sándwich?", pregunta.

"Oh, ese es mi favorito", dice la Reina. "Sándwich de **ensalada** de puerros."

"Oh, puerros", dice Úrsula. Se siente enferma. La Reina alcanza a uno. Ella toma un bocado.

"Toma uno, querida", dice la Reina.

"Gracias, Su Majestad", dice Ursula. Ella toma un sándwich de puerros. Puede sentir que su estómago se revuelve. Ella toma un bocado enorme porque está muy nerviosa. Su cara se vuelve blanca, luego verde.

"¿Estás bien, querida?" pregunta la Reina. "Te ves muy mal."

"E- E- Estoy bien", dice Ursula. Siente que su estómago se revuelve. Siente que va a vomitar. No puede impedir que los puerros vuelvan a subir por su garganta. Al menos siguió las otras reglas para almorzar con la Reina, piensa. Nadie dijo nada sobre vómitos.

RESUMEN

Ursula es una niña. Vive en Londres, Inglaterra. Está obsesionada con la familia real. Cena con su madre y ve la televisión. En la TV, anuncian un concurso. La ganadora almuerza con la propia Reina. Entra Úrsula. Al día siguiente, en el desayuno, anuncian al ganador. ¡Es Úrsula! Ella va al Palacio de Buckingham para el almuerzo. Ella sigue las reglas para comer con la Reina. La Reina ha preparado sándwiches especiales. Desafortunadamente, la ensalada de puerros no es la comida favorita de Ursula. Se siente enferma mientras ve a la Reina comerse el sándwich.

Lista de Vocabulario

is	es / está
has	ha / has
to be	ser / estar
have	tener
are	eres / estás
leeks	puerros
am	soy / estoy
vegetable	vegetales

carrot	zanahoria
broccoli	brócoli
salad	ensalada
lunch	almuerzo
have to	tener que
dessert	postre
grapes	uvas
cherries	cerezas
fruit	fruta
cream	crema
sugar	azúcar
meal	comida
breakfast	desayuno
cereal	cereal
egg	huevo
bacon	tocino

sandwiches	sándwiches
tea	té
ham	jamón
cheese	queso
mustard	mostaza
cookies	galletas
scones	bollos
salad	ensalada

PREGUNTAS

1) ¿Qué pasa cuando Ursula prueba los puerros por primera vez?

    a) ella los ama

    b) su madre los quema

    c) ella casi vomita

    d) no se da cuenta

2) ¿Cuál es la regla cuando comes con la Reina de Inglaterra?

    a) no debes comer hasta que ella coma

    b) debes usar azul

    c) debes comer sándwiches

    d) debes sentarte antes que ella

3) ¿Qué piensa la madre de Úrsula sobre el concurso?

    a) Ursula tiene la oportunidad de ganar

    b) es una falsificación

    c) la Reina no debe estar involucrada

    d) Ursula nunca ganará

4) ¿Qué tiene para comer la Reina?

    a) un buen asado

    b) salmón, su favorito

c) galletas de té y sándwiches

d) es ultra secreto

5) ¿Cuál de las siguientes afirmaciones es cierta?

a) Úrsula huye en medio del almuerzo

b) Ursula no puede controlar su reacción a los puerros

c) la Reina hizo los sándwiches ella misma

d) los sándwiches no son buena comida para el almuerzo

RESPUESTAS

1) ¿Qué pasa cuando Ursula prueba los puerros por primera vez?

c) ella casi vomita

2) ¿Cuál es la regla cuando comes con la Reina de Inglaterra?

a) no debes comer hasta que ella coma

3) ¿Qué piensa la madre de Úrsula sobre el concurso?

d) Ursula nunca ganará

4) ¿Qué tiene para comer la Reina?

c) galletas de té y sándwiches

5) ¿Cuál de las siguientes afirmaciones es cierta?

b) Ursula no puede controlar su reacción a los puerros

Translation of the Story

Lunch with The Queen

STORY

Ursula **is** a young girl. She lives in London, England. She studies at school. She loves to bake. She **has** an obsession: the royal family. She wants **to be** a princess.

One night, Ursula is at home. Her mother prepares her dinner. They **have** something new. Her mother brings the plate to the table.

"What **are** those?" asks Ursula.

"These are **leeks**," says Ursula's mom.

"Oh, I don't like leeks," says Ursula.

"Try them," says her mom. She tries them. She almost vomits.

"I **am** sick," says Ursula.

"No, you are not," says her mom.

"Please, give me any other **vegetable**," says Ursula. "**Carrots, broccoli, salad**?"

"Oh, Ursula, just eat your **meat** then," says her mom. She turns on the television. They watch the news. The report is about the Queen of England. Ursula stops eating. She pays close attention.

"Queen Elizabeth reigns in England for 68 years," says the news report. "She is married to Prince Phillip. They have four children."

The news report talks about the Queen. She lives in Buckingham Palace. She is very healthy, despite her age.

"I want to visit Buckingham Palace," says Ursula.

"Yes, dear," says her mom. They watch the program. The program announces a special competition. One person can win a visit to Buckingham Palace. The winner will eat **lunch** with the queen. Ursula screams.

"I **have to** win!" she shouts.

"I don't know," says her mom. "Many people enter the contest."

Ursula watches the program. She learns how to enter. She takes a picture of herself eating. Then she posts it on social media. She watches the program, which talks about eating with the Queen. She watches as they show what happened to a prince from the South Pacific.

The Queen is on a boat with the prince. They serve **dessert**. The prince forgets to watch the Queen. He takes some **grapes** and some **cherries** from the **fruit** on the table and puts them in his bowl. He pours **cream** over them. He sprinkles **sugar** on top. He starts to eat, and then he realizes the Queen has not. He makes a big mistake. The Queen takes her spoon. She eats a bit. That makes the prince feel better. He is very embarrassed.

"There are rules to eat with the Queen?" she asks her mom.

"Of course," says her mom.

"Like what?" asks Ursula.

"Well, the Queen begins the **meal** and ends the meal," says Ursula's mom.

"You mean you can't eat until she does," says Ursula.

"That's right," says her mom. "And when she finishes, you finish, too."

"What if you aren't finished?" asks Ursula.

"You are," says her mom. "And you must wait for the Queen to sit."

"Before you sit?" says Ursula.

"Right," says her mom. Ursula thinks about this. There are lots of rules if you are queen or princess. Ursula and her mom finish dinner. They go to sleep.

The next morning, Ursula wakes up. She is nervous about the contest. Today they announce the winner. She eats **breakfast** with her mom.

"I am nervous," she says.

"Ursula, you won't win," says her mom. "So many people are in the contest."

"Oh," says Ursula. She is sad. She eats her **cereal**. She is not hungry. Her **bacon** and **eggs** sit untouched.

They turn on the television.

"And we announce the winner of the Lunch with the Queen Contest," says the man on the TV. He puts his hand into a huge glass bowl full of papers. He moves his hand around. He pulls out a paper. He opens the paper.

"And the winner is…Ursula Vann!" he says.

Ursula looks at her mom. Her mom looks at her.

"Did you hear that?" she asks. Her mom nods, staring. Her mouth is open.

"Did I win?" she asks. Her mom nods, speechless.

"Woo-hoo!" shouts Ursula. "I knew I would! I'm going to see the queen!" Ursula finishes her food and goes to school.

The next day is the day for lunch with the Queen. Ursula walks up to the palace. She is terrified. She is only a young girl. This is a big adventure for such a young girl.

"Who are you?" asks a guard.

"Ursula Vann," she says. "I won the contest to have lunch with the Queen."

"Oh, hello, young lady," the guard says. "You are a pretty young lass. Come in."

"Thank you," she says.

A guard takes her to the palace. It is grand, and very big. They walk through the halls. The guard has a funny hat. Ursula giggles. Then, she stops. They are in the dining room.

The Queen of England is sitting at the table! There is a plate of **sandwiches** in front of her. She is small. She is happy, and she is smiling.

"Hello, dear," she says.

"Hello, your majesty," Ursula says. She courtsies.

"Thank you for coming to lunch," she says.

"It is my pleasure, your **Majesty**," says Ursula.

"I hope you don't mind. We will be having **tea** instead of a proper lunch," says the Queen. She sits again. Ursula remembers her manners. She sits, too.

The sandwiches are royal sandwiches, she thinks. They look a lot like sandwiches from home, though. Some have **ham** and **cheese**, with a yellow bit of **mustard**. Others have a **mayonnaise** salad on them. There is a plate of **cookies** next to some **scones**.

"Pardon me, your Majesty," says Ursula.

"Yes, dear?" says the Queen.

"What is on that sandwich?" she asks.

"Oh, that's my favorite," says the Queen. "Leek **salad** sandwich."

"Oh, leeks," says Ursula. She feels sick. The Queen reaches for one. She takes a bite.

"Have one, dear," says the Queen.

"Thank you, your Majesty," says Ursula. She takes a leek sandwich. She can feel her stomach turn. She takes a huge bite because she is so nervous. Her face turns white, then green.

"Are you alright, dear?" asks the Queen. "You look quite unwell."

"I- I- I'm fine," says Ursula. She feels her stomach turning. She feels as if she will vomit. She can't stop the leeks from coming back up her throat. At least she followed the other rules for eating lunch with the Queen, she thinks. Nobody ever said anything about vomiting.

www.LearnLikeNatives.com

CONCLUSION

You did it!

You finished a whole book in a brand new language. That in and of itself is quite the accomplishment, isn't it?

Congratulate yourself on time well spent and a job well done. Now that you've finished the book, you have familiarized yourself with over 500 new vocabulary words, comprehended the heart of 3 short stories, and listened to loads of dialogue unfold, all without going anywhere!

Charlemagne said "To have another language is to possess a second soul." After immersing yourself in this book, you are broadening your horizons and opening a whole new path for yourself.

Have you thought about how much you know now that you did not know before? You've learned everything from how to greet and how to express your emotions to basics like colors and place words. You can tell time and ask question. All without opening a schoolbook. Instead, you've cruised through fun, interesting stories and possibly listened to them as well.

Perhaps before you weren't able to distinguish meaning when you listened to Spanish. If you used the audiobook, we bet you can now pick out meanings and words when you hear someone speaking. Regardless, we are sure you have taken an important step to being more fluent. You are well on your way!

Best of all, you have made the essential step of distinguishing in your mind the idea that most often hinders people studying a new language. By approaching Spanish through our short stories and dialogs, instead of formal lessons with just grammar and vocabulary, you are no longer in the 'learning' mindset. Your approach is much more similar to an osmosis, focused on speaking and using the language, which is the end goal, after all!

So, what's next?

This is just the first of five books, all packed full of short stories and dialogs, covering essential, everyday Spanish that will ensure you master the basics. You can find the rest of the books in the series, as well as a whole host of other resources, at LearnLikeNatives.com. Simply add the book to your library to take the next step in your language learning journey. If you are ever in need of new ideas or direction, refer to our 'Speak Like a Native' eBook, available to you for free at LearnLikeNatives.com, which clearly outlines practical steps you can take to continue learning any language you choose.

We also encourage you to get out into the real world and practice your Spanish. You have a leg up on most beginners, after all—instead of pure textbook learning, you have been absorbing the sound and soul of the language. Do not underestimate the foundation you have built reviewing the chapters of this book. Remember, no one feels 100% confident when they speak with a native speaker in another language.

One of the coolest things about being human is connecting with others. Communicating with someone in their own language is a wonderful gift. Knowing the language turns you into a local and opens up your world. You will see the reward of learning languages for many years to come, so keep that practice up!. Don't let your fears stop you from taking the chance to use your Spanish. Just give it a try, and remember that you will make mistakes. However, these mistakes will teach you so much, so view every single one as a small victory! Learning is growth.

www.LearnLikeNatives.com

Don't let the quest for learning end here! There is so much you can do to continue the learning process in an organic way, like you did with this book. Add another book from Learn Like a Native to your library. Listen to Spanish talk radio. Watch some of the great Spanish films. Put on the latest

CD from Rosalia. Take salsa lessons in Spanish. Whatever you do, don't stop because every little

step you take counts towards learning a new language, culture, and way of communicating.

www.LearnLikeNatives.com

www.LearnLikeNatives.com

Learn Like a Native is a revolutionary **language education brand** that is taking the linguistic world by storm. Forget boring grammar books that never get you anywhere, Learn Like a Native teaches you languages in a fast and fun way that actually works!

As an international, multichannel, language learning platform, we provide **books, audio guides and eBooks** so that you can acquire the knowledge you need, swiftly and easily.

Our **subject-based learning**, structured around real-world scenarios, builds your conversational muscle and ensures you learn the content most relevant to your requirements. Discover our tools at *LearnLikeNatives.com*.

When it comes to learning languages, we've got you covered!

www.ingramcontent.com/pod-product-compliance
Lightning Source LLC
Chambersburg PA
CBHW071743080526
44588CB00013B/2139